Hi. My name is Inti, and I'm a jaguar. I live in the Amazon rainforest with my sister and mama. Even though I'm young, I've had a lot of adventures.

Come with me, and I'll tell you our story.

Early one summer morning, as the first light appeared in the sky, my sister was born. Mama named her Chasca, after the goddess of the dawn.

As the sun began to rise in the sky, I arrived. Mama named me Inti, after the powerful sun god.

For two weeks, our eyes stayed closed. Mama kept us warm in our cave and fed us her milk.

The day our eyes opened, Chasca and I looked at each other and growled. We've been best friends ever since.

Chasca and I liked our home in the cave.

One day, Mama surprised us. "You two are bigger and stronger now," she said. "Would you like to see the forest outside?"

Excited, Chasca and I jumped on Mama. "When? Now? Can we go now?"

"Tomorrow," Mama said. "I'll take you tomorrow."

"This," Mama said, "is our forest home."

"Wow!" Chasca said. "Look at all the colors!"

"It's so big!" I said. "Look at all the trees to climb! Are we the only ones who live here?"

A flock of parrots flew overhead, making loud screeching sounds. "Braaaaaak! Braaaaaak!"

Mama laughed. "Inti, more animals live in this forest than you could ever count."

"Mama, how long before I am as big as you?" I asked.

"About two summers," Mama said, "and then you will be bigger than me."

"How long does it take for the trees to grow up?" Chasca asked. "They're so tall!"

"Some of these trees grow tall in ten summers," Mama said. "The giant trees grow for thousands of summers."

"Thousands of summers! Whoa!" Chasca said, surprised.

"I hear a strange noise," I interrupted, looking up past the trees.

"Oh, no," Mama said. "A sky machine! That means danger."

"But we're jaguars. Nobody messes with us!" I said.

"Nobody except men," Mama warned. "Back into the cave! Quick!"

From the entrance of our cave, Mama watched and listened. Sky machines and land machines roared in the distance. Huge trees fell, one after another.

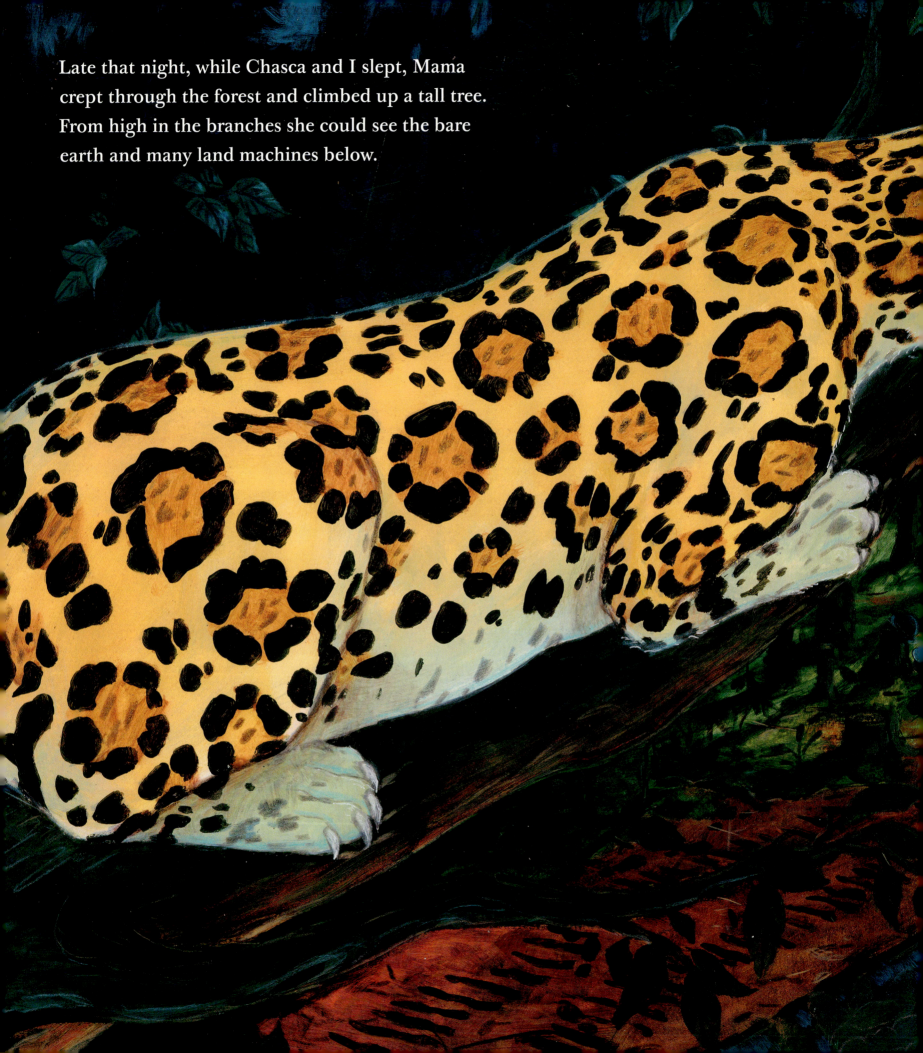

Late that night, while Chasca and I slept, Mama crept through the forest and climbed up a tall tree. From high in the branches she could see the bare earth and many land machines below.

As night ended and the sun rose, the forest remained quiet. "How many birds had to fly away to find new homes?" Mama wondered aloud. "And what about the rest of us? Where will all the land animals go?"

After waking up and not finding Mama, Chasca and I left the cave to look for her.

"What have we got here?" said a big man, pointing a shiny stick at us. Chasca and I froze, too surprised to run away.
"I thought you jaguars were extinct. Go find your mama and get out of here before you get yourselves killed."

As soon as the man left, Mama rushed to us from her hiding place and pulled us into the safety of our cave.

"Mama," Chasca asked, "What does extinct mean?"

"It means gone," Mama answered. "Gone from the earth."

"Does extinct mean forever? I asked. "Gone forever?"

"Yes," Mama said.

Chasca and I looked at each other, horrified.

"But we are not going extinct!" Mama said, shaking her head. "We will find a new home, far from here, where there are no men or machines. Let me rest now, and we'll leave tonight."

That night we said goodbye to our home and started on our journey. Traveling by the light of the moon, Mama spoke about our history.

"In the past," she said, "men and women honored jaguars. The forest people knew we brought them good fortune, so they never harmed us.

"We lived in this great forest together. They enjoyed watching us hunt, and admired our strength and speed.

"That was a long time ago," Mama said sadly. "Now we must avoid them."

"Mama! I can see the river from up here," I said.
"I'm so thirsty. Can I run ahead?"

"No. We stay together," Mama reminded me.

Chasca and I got the shock of our lives when we arrived at the river. The trees lay on their sides, uprooted. In the river, the colorful fish no longer swam.

Angry, Chasca asked, "What happened to the trees? And what happened to the river? Why are all the fish dead?"

"Men have been here, digging for gold rocks," Mama said. Her eyes filled with tears. "They pour something into the water that acts like poison, killing everything. We'll have to go upriver to drink."

We traveled many days and many nights on our journey to find a new home. Mama continued teaching us everything a jaguar needs to know to stay safe in the rainforest.

Chasca and I continued to grow bigger and stronger. My growl got bigger, too.

One day, I smelled trees burning. I ran ahead to see if there was a forest fire.

As far as we could see, rows of plants covered the land. Thousands of strange animals huddled together in the distance.

"Who are those poor animals?" Chasca asked. "And why is there fire and smoke over there?"

"Those are cows," Mama said, "brought here from other lands. The forest is cut and burned to grow food for them."

"Mama! Look over there!" Chasca warned. "Men on horses are coming this way!"

"Inti, Chasca, listen closely," Mama told us. "It's time to practice what I've taught you. Become invisible to others and travel silently."

For the rest of that day and into the night, we followed Mama without making a sound. We passed many ranches and farms, invisible to the men and their horses.

That night, no one, not even the moon and the stars, could see us.

A few nights later, Mama and I awoke to Chasca crying.

"Mama," Chasca said, "in my nightmare, the forest was dying. Land machines and sky machines were everywhere. The animals had nowhere to live and nowhere to hide."

Wiping her tears with her paw, Chasca whispered, "Mama, I'm scared. Is anywhere safe for us?"

Mama pulled us close and licked our heads to comfort us. "We'll be safe soon," she said. "It won't be long before we find a new home."

Reassured, Chasca and I snuggled together and quickly fell asleep.

"It's raining especially hard today," I said, looking up at the clouds.

"I like the rain," Chasca said.
"I can drink from the sky and play in the puddles."

"Yes, but can you wrestle with your brother?" I challenged her.

Without saying a word, Chasca tackled me, and we rolled around wrestling in the mud, laughing and growling.

Early the next morning, as the sun rose in the sky, the storm clouds began to clear.

"Listen, Chasca! Listen, Inti!" Mama said. "Do you hear all the monkeys?"

"Yes! And parrots!" I said.

"I see giant trees," Chasca said. "Mama, did we make it?"

"Yes!" Mama said, smiling. "We made it!"

Our journey to find a new home was long and sometimes scary. But it was worth it.

"I like everything about our new home," Chasca said.

"Me, too!" I said.

"Me, three!" Mama said, and we all purred.

We're safe now, and we get to sleep in the trees with the moon and the stars shining down on us.

"Sweet dreams, Chasca," Mama said. "Sweet dreams, Inti."

MORE ABOUT JAGUARS
(Panthera onca)

AT BIRTH

Mother jaguars give birth to one to four cubs. Most often, two cubs are born.

A newborn jaguar cub weighs only 1½–2 pounds (700–900 g). About 5 newborn kittens together weigh what a newborn jaguar weighs.

The jaguar cub's eyes are sealed shut for 10–14 days after birth.

Jaguar cubs stay with their mother for about two years. She protects them from danger and teaches them how to hunt.

FULLY GROWN

Female jaguars weigh 100–200 pounds (45–90 kg). Male jaguars weigh 125–250 pounds (57–113 kg).

From nose to tail a full-grown jaguar is 6 to 8 feet in length (1.8–2.4 m).

A jaguar's lifespan is estimated to be 12–15 years in the wild. Jaguars who live on reserves often live 15–20 years.

Jaguars are the largest big cats that live in the Americas, and the 3rd largest big cat in the world.

No two jaguars look exactly alike. Every jaguar has her or his own unique spots and rosettes.

DID YOU KNOW?

Jaguars have a layer of tissue in the back of their eyes that reflect light. They can see 6 times better than you or I can at night or in dark places.

Jaguars like water and are good swimmers. They swim in freshwater lakes and rivers. They hunt in the water too.

Jaguars hear really well too, and their sense of smell is strong.

Jaguars make a variety of sounds, including hissing, mewing, grunting, and roaring.

Jaguars often sleep in the branches of a tree. They like to eat up in the trees too.

JAGUARS, LEOPARDS & PANTHERS

There are eight subspecies of jaguars, which vary in their size and coloring. Jaguars and leopards look very similar, but live far away from one another, on different continents. Black panthers are really black jaguars (or black leopards in Asia). If you look closely you will see rosettes on the skin underneath their fur.

WHERE DO JAGUARS LIVE?

Today most jaguars are found in South America, near rivers or swamps. The Amazon rainforest is their primary habitat. Some jaguars also live in Central America and Mexico. Occasionally a jaguar is spotted in the southern United States.

Since 1997 jaguars have been listed as an endangered species. Wildlife experts estimate that only 10,000–15,000 jaguars exist in the wild today.

There are many ways you can help protect jaguars and the Amazon rainforest. Find out more at TheJaguarsStory.org

Amazon Rainforest Fauna and Flora

How many of these rainforest residents can you find in *The Jaguar's Story*?

MAMMALS

Armadillos are an odd looking mammal that have an armor-like covering on their back, head, legs, and tail. In the rainforest there are many varieties. The smallest are only 6 inches in length (15 cm), and the biggest grow 5 feet long (1.5 m).

Bats, more than 100 species, live in the Amazon rainforest. Bats are the only pollinators of many of the fruit trees such as kapok, cashew, mango, banana, avocado, guava, and durian, and of hardwood trees such as ebony and mahogany.

Capuchin Monkeys are known for being very intelligent and adaptable, and have been used as trained actors in movies and for pets. But capuchin monkeys would rather live in the rainforest with their friends and family than be a movie star.

Giant Anteaters can grow 7 feet long (2 m) from snout to tail. They have no teeth but they eat as many as 35,000 ants and termites a day! How? They use their long tongues to suck up the insects quickly and swallow them whole. They can stand on their hind legs and with their 4 inch claws (10 cm) fight off a jaguar or puma.

Golden Lion Tamarin Monkeys get their name from the long reddish-gold hairs framing their face like a lion's mane. They are quite small, only 8–14 inches tall (20–36 cm), and weigh only 1–2 pounds (450–900 g).

Milton's Titi Monkeys have a reddish-orange tail and reddish-orange hair around their face, with a light gray stripe on their forehead. Like other titi monkeys, they find their life-long

mate around 4 years of age, and the couple rear their young together.

Sloths spend most of their life in the rainforest canopy, using vines to travel about to find food. In an entire day sloths move only about 40 yards (37 m) and then sleep for 15 hours. Their long, curved claws make it possible for them to hang upside down from tree branches.

Spider Monkeys got their name from the funny way they hang from the trees. They have a powerful tail they wrap around branches while the rest of their body dangles. With their long arms they can travel quickly through the forest, swinging from tree to tree. Spider monkeys like to gather in large groups in the canopy, loudly chattering with one another.

BIRDS

Blue and Yellow Macaws, and **Scarlet Macaws** are large parrots with colorful feathers, long tails, sharp beaks, and strong talons (feet). Flocks of macaws, often with 100 birds or more, are amazing to see in flight. You can hear their loud squawks from far, far away!

Blue-fronted Parrots are green with yellow faces and bright blue feathers on their forehead. These parrots live in flocks, and once they choose their mate, they do everything as a couple: they eat together, sleep together, and raise their young together.

Campo Flicker Woodpeckers have golden yellow faces and a black crown and neck. When they spread their wings to fly you can see their unique brown and white patterned feathers. These woodpeckers forage for food on the forest floor, eating termites, ants and beetles.

Masked Trogon birds are the only animal with two toes facing back and two toes facing forward. When they find a fruit they want to eat, they hover before it and pluck at it. Masked trogons make lots of funny noises that sound like whistles and barks.

Scarlet Ibis birds have beautiful bright red feathers with black tips, and pinkish-red legs and feet. Quite tall, they are strong flyers and can travel far distances. They live in flocks of 30 or more, and choose their mate for life.

Toucans are large birds famous for their bright colored faces and long, banana shaped bills. Toucans jump from branch to branch high in the canopy, picking fruits and swallowing them whole. Sometimes they play catch, tossing berries with their long bills to their mates.

Wattled Jacana birds live in wetlands and are able to walk on floating vegetation with their large webbed toes and claws. The females have several mates, and the males incubate the eggs.

Green Anacondas are the largest snakes in the world, growing 20–30 feet long (6–9 m), 12 inches around (30 cm), and weighing as much as 550 pounds (227 kg). Because their eyes and nostrils are on the top of their head, they can see and breathe while most of their body lies hidden in the water. Female anacondas give birth to 30 or more live snakes at a time. Each are 1–2 feet long at birth (30–60 cm) and live for 10–30 years.

Poison Dart Frogs come in a variety of bright, florescent body colors: blue, orange, red, yellow, green, and copper. Dart frogs are small, only ½ inch to 2 inches long (1.3–5 cm). They are one of the most poisonous creatures in the world – but not all of them. Some dart frogs are harmless.

REPTILES AND AMPHIBIANS

The **Rainbow Boa** is a reddish-brown snake with 3 black stripes on its head and large black rings down its back. Its colorful, iridescent sheen comes from small ridges on its scales that refract light and create a prism or rainbow of colors.

Caiman are in the crocodilian family and have no enemies in the Amazon accept jaguars and men. Even though caiman have sharp, pointed teeth, a mother caiman gently carries her newly hatched young in her mouth, bringing them, one by one, from their nest to shallow waters.

Yellow-spotted Turtles live in fresh water lakes, lagoons and rivers. During the day they like to warm themselves in the sun. These turtles do not pull their neck and head directly back into their shell, but tuck them to one side.

INSECTS

The **Blue Morpho Butterfly,** with a wingspan of 5–8 inches (13–20 cm) is one of the largest butterflies in the world. The male blue morphos have shimmering metallic blue wings that face the sky, and their underside wings are brown, red, and black with eyespots that camouflage them. When they fly their wings flash from bright blue to dull brown, making it look like they appear and then disappear, over and over again.

Brazilian Wandering Spiders or banana spiders are the most venomous spiders in the world. With their long legs they move quickly when hunting at night, and hide during the day. They have red jaws and 8 eyes!

Fireflies are winged beetles that emit their own flashing light at twilight and at night. Most varieties of fireflies (there are about 2,000) like warm, humid climates.

Hawk Moths and hummingbirds are about the same size, and both hover while drinking nectar from flowers with their long tongues. Hawk moths also hum while they eat.

Jewel Caterpillars are tiny creatures, ½ inch long (1.3 cm) that appear to have jewels set in their semi-translucent projections. These projections come off easily when a predator attempts to eat them, becoming goo in their mouth. Unharmed, the caterpillar has time to escape. There are 80 species of jewel caterpillars, each with its own amazing colors and patterns.

Leafcutter Ants have unique mandibles that act like a saw to easily cut leaves and flowers. The ants carry their cuttings back to their nest and use these plants to grow their own food in underground fungus farms. Leafcutter ants have the largest societies in the animal and insect world: their nests house 10–20 million ants!

Leaf Insects look so much like leaves they are really hard to spot when they are on the leaves of plants or trees. Their extraordinary camouflage protects them from being eaten.

Scarlet Peacock Butterflies are often seen in groups of 50 or more. Their brilliant red, black and white wings for males, or orange, brown, and white for females, span 1½ inches (4 cm). They like to bask in the sun, and will fly in light rain showers. In the early evening they roost together upside down, wings closed, on the underside of leaves.

TREES AND FLOWERS

Açai Palm Trees grow 50–100 feet tall (15–30 m) along river banks and wetlands. The flavorful fruits that grow on these palm trees, known as açai berries, look like dark purple grapes.

Amazon Giant Water Lilies are the world's largest lily flower and lily pads. The white lily flowers, which turn dark pink after being pollinated, are as large as a soccer ball. The lily pads grow up to 6 feet across (1.8 m) and are strong enough to hold you and a friend. Each plant produces 40–50 of these enormous lily pad leaves, but only one flower.

Cacao Trees produce green, red and purplish fruits that grow from its trunk and large branches. As these fruits ripen their color turns to yellow and orange. Inside are large seeds that are the source of cacao, or cocoa. Chocolate is made from the cocoa powder and cocoa butter from these seeds.

Cupuacu Trees produce delicious large melon sized fruits that are brown and fuzzy on the outside, with a creamy white pulp on the inside.

Jaboticaba Trees produce white flowers and grape-like fruits that grow directly from the trunk of the tree.

Orchids, many thousands of different species, grow abundantly in the rainforest. While some orchids grow in the soil, most grow on trees and plants, and some grow on rocks! Each orchid species has a different bird or insect pollinator. The singing orchid, discovered in Peru in 2014, sing to attract their pollinator: hummingbirds.

White Passion Flowers grow on woody vines that attach themselves to other plants and trees. The flowers, leaves, and fruits of this vine are valued for their beauty, flavor, and medicinal properties.

Discover more Amazon Rainforest Fauna and Flora, Children's Activity pages, Art lessons, Wildlife video links, and more, at **TheJaguarsStory.org**

FROM THE AUTHOR

The names I chose for the jaguars are from the Quechua - Inca language.

Inti is the name for the sun, the rising sun, and for the sun god. In Incan folklore Inti gave rainbows to the people to provide them a road from the earth to the sky.

Chasca is the name for the goddess of the dawn and twilight, and the planet Venus. In Incan folklore Chasca is a goddess of love and light. Her light enables flowers to grow and she transforms negative energy into positive.

Suyana, the name I chose for Mama jaguar, means hope, or to hope. In this story Suyana exhibits great inner strength and determination to protect her cubs, never giving up hope that a better life awaits them.

I wrote this book with the hope *The Jaguar's Story* spurs a revolution to protect jaguars and halt destruction of the Amazon rainforest.

Please visit me at www.KosaEly.com

FROM THE ILLUSTRATOR

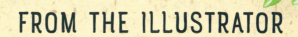

I enjoyed creating the visual world of this book, and learned so much about jaguars and the Amazon rainforest in the process.

Inti, Chasca, and Mama each have their own unique spots and markings on their faces, necks, and coats. See if you can "spot" them.

My young son watched me sketch and paint these illustrations over the past year. He can find all the animals and insects in the illustrations. See if you can find them too.

The more I learn about the animals and plants of the rainforest, the more concerned I am to protect them from harm. Please join me in bringing *The Jaguar's Story* to as many families as possible, and doing all we can to protect the Amazon rainforest and the animals who live there.

Please visit me at
www.RadheGendron.com

To my Dad, and our clan, with love.
—*Kosa*

To my sweet son Kirtan,
and all the curious children in the world.
—*Radhe*

Thank you to our generous sponsors:

Ever grateful to Bimala Naysmith, Bada Haridas, Nitai Ely, Gaura Ely, and Pranada Comtois (Inword Publishers).

Summary: Deep in the Amazon, two cubs are born to a loving mama jaguar. Before long their happy days are interrupted by men and machines. Afraid for their lives, the young family goes in search of a new home. Join them to discover the wonders and dangers of today's Amazon rainforest through the eyes of a jaguar.

Chandra Media
Gainesville, Florida
www.chandramedia.org

Text copyright © 2018 Kosa Ely
Illustrations copyright © 2018 Radhe Gendron
Book design by Govinda Cordua
All rights reserved. No part of this book may be reproduced in any form without written permission from the publisher.
ISBN 978-0-9996654-0-4
Library of Congress Control Number: 2018900770
Printed in Canada on FSC certified paper with vegetable inks.